To:

_____

From:

_____

Published by Barbour Publishing, Inc., P.O. Box 719, Uhrichsville, Ohio 44683, www.barbourbooks.com

Cover and Interior Design: Thinkpen Design, Inc., www.thinkpendesign.com

Our mission is to publish and distribute inspirational products offering exceptional value and biblical encouragement to the masses.

Member of the
Evangelical Christian
Publishers Association

Printed in China.

The Real Gift of Christmas

Music & Inspiration to Celebrate the Season

BARBOUR
PUBLISHING

For unto us a child is born,
unto us a son is given: and the
government shall be upon his
shoulder: and his name shall be
called Wonderful, Counsellor,
The mighty God, The everlasting
Father, The Prince of Peace.

Isaiah 9:6 kjv

What a strange way for God to come to us—
as a helpless, vulnerable baby! No wonder so
many people alive at the time of His coming
completely missed what had happened;
they were expecting something far different.
God still has a way of doing that: He comes to
us in unexpected ways, in small ways, in ways
we may overlook if we're too busy to pay
attention. But whether we notice Him or not,
He is always present with us.
Look for the Christ Child's presence in your Life.
You may find Him where you least expect Him.

*And she brought forth
her firstborn son, and wrapped
him in swaddling clothes,
and laid him in a manger.*

LUKE 2:7 KJV

At Christmastime, we celebrate the birth of Jesus of Nazareth, a baby who was born more than two thousand years ago. Caught up in the season's bright lights and frantic busyness, we may lose sight of the child whose birthday we celebrate. . . .

But Christmas means far more than tinsel
and evergreen and pretty packages. The true
meaning of our celebration is this:
The child who was born so long ago
came because He loves you.
He wants to give Himself to you.
He was born for you.

When they saw the star, they were overjoyed. . . . They saw the child with his mother Mary, and they bowed down and worshiped him. Then they opened their treasures and presented him with gifts.

MATTHEW 2:10–11 NIV

And by the light of that same star,
Three wise men came from country far,
To seek for a king was their intent,
And to follow the star wherever it went. . . .

This star drew nigh to the northwest,
O'er Bethlehem it took its rest;
And there it did both stop and stay,
Right over the place where Jesus lay.

TRADITIONAL ENGLISH CAROL

*And she shall bring forth a son,
and thou shalt call his name JESUS:
for he shall save his people from their sins.*

MATTHEW 1:21 KJV

Born thy people
to deliver,
Born a child and
yet a King,
Born to reign in
us forever,
Now thy gracious
kingdom bring.

CHARLES WESLEY

Are you willing to believe that love is the strongest thing in the world—stronger than hate, stronger than evil, stronger than death—and that the blessed life which began in Bethlehem nineteen hundred years ago is the image and brightness of the eternal love? Then you can keep Christmas.

HENRY VAN DYKE

And suddenly there was with the angel a multitude of the heavenly host praising God, and saying, Glory to God in the highest, and on earth peace, good will toward men. And it came to pass, as the angels were gone away from them into heaven, the shepherds said one to another, Let us now go even unto Bethlehem, and see this thing which is come to pass, which the Lord hath made known unto us.

LUKE 2:13–15 KJV

This day and your life are God's gifts to you: so give thanks and be joyful always!

Jim Beggs

At this special time of year,
may you share the wisdom the
wise men knew so long ago...may
you sense the presence of the
Christ Child in your life.

ELLYN SANNA WITH
VIOLA RUELKE GOMMER

"Glory to God in the highest heaven, and on earth peace to those on whom his favor rests."

LUKE 2:14 NIV

We hear the Christmas angels
The great glad tidings tell;
O come to us, abide with us,
Our Lord Emmanuel.

PHILLIPS BROOKS

Sometimes the Christ Child
seems completely absent from our
world. Innocence, love, and joy are
sadly missing. We cannot even
find Him in our own hearts.
But He is still there. Sin hides Him
from our sight…but the sun still
shines behind the clouds, and Christ
is always present in our lives….

I pray that you will see Him this
Christmas season.

ELLYN SANNA WITH
VIOLA RUELKE GOMMER

But the angel said to them, "Do not be afraid. I bring you good news that will cause great joy for all the people."

LUKE 2:10 NIV

Love came down at Christmas,
Love all lovely, love divine;
Love was born at Christmas;
Star and angels gave the sign.

CHRISTINA ROSSETTI

Good news from heaven the angels bring,
Glad tidings to the earth they sing:
To us this day a child is given,
To crown us with the joy of heaven.

MARTIN LUTHER

The Son is the image of the invisible God, the firstborn over all creation.

Colossians 1:15 niv

Jesus did not come to make
God's love possible, but to
make God's love visible.

UNKNOWN

Peace I leave with you; my peace I give you. I do not give to you as the world gives. Do not let your hearts be troubled and do not be afraid.

JESUS OF NAZARETH
(FROM JOHN 14:27 NIV)

The Christ Child's life was a present to us from God, the present of His very self. Jesus came to our earth, bringing us eternal gifts from heaven. One of the best of these gifts is the peace of God, the peace Jesus wants you to experience in your own life.

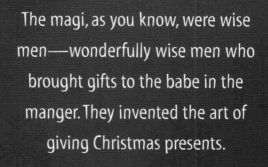

The magi, as you know, were wise men—wonderfully wise men who brought gifts to the babe in the manger. They invented the art of giving Christmas presents.

O. HENRY

What can I give him, poor as I am?
If I were a shepherd, I would give him a lamb.
If I were a wise man, I would do my part—
Yet what can I give Him? Give my heart.

Christina Rossetti

And there were in the same country shepherds abiding in the field, keeping watch over their flock by night. And, lo, the angel of the Lord came upon them, and the glory of the Lord shone round about them: and they were sore afraid. And the angel said unto them, Fear not: for, behold, I bring you good tidings of great joy, which shall be to all people. For unto you is born this day in the city of David a Saviour, which is Christ the Lord.

LUKE 2:8–11 KJV

On Christmas Day two thousand years ago, the birth of a tiny baby in an obscure village in the Middle East was God's supreme triumph of good over evil.

CHARLES COLSON

But when the fulness of the time was come, God sent forth his Son.

GALATIANS 4:4 KJV

Joy to the world, the Lord is come!
Let earth receive her King;
Let every heart prepare Him room,
And heaven and nature sing. . . .

Joy to the earth, the Savior reigns!
Let men their songs employ;
While fields and floods,
rocks, hills, and plains,
Repeat the sounding joy.

ISAAC WATTS

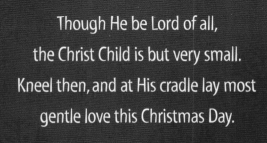

Though He be Lord of all,
the Christ Child is but very small.
Kneel then, and at His cradle lay most
gentle love this Christmas Day.

ANONYMOUS

And the Word was made flesh,
and dwelt among us,
(and we beheld his glory).

JOHN 1:14 KJV

The birth of the baby Jesus stands
as the most significant event in all
history, because it has meant the
pouring into a sick world of the
healing medicine of love which has
transformed all manner of hearts
for almost two thousand years.

George Matthew Adams

As the centuries pass the evidence is accumulating that, measured by His effect on history, Jesus is the most influential life ever lived on this planet.

KENNETH SCOTT LATOURETTE

All this took place to fulfill what the Lord had said through the prophet: "The virgin will conceive and give birth to a son, and they will call him Immanuel" (which means "God with us").

MATTHEW 1:22–23 NIV

Jesus came!—and came for me.
Simple words! and yet expressing
Depths of holy mystery,
Depths of wondrous love and blessing.
Holy Spirit, make me see
All His coming means to me;
Take the things of Christ, I pray,
Show them to my heart today.

FRANCES RIDLEY HAVERGAL

The second person in God, the Son, became human Himself: was born into the world as an actual man—a real man of a particular height, with hair of a particular color, speaking a particular language. . . the eternal being, who knows everything and who created the whole universe, became not only a man but (before that) a baby. . . . The Son of God became a man to enable men to become sons of God.

C. S. Lewis

O come, let us worship and bow down: let us kneel before the LORD our maker.

PSALM 95:6 KJV

Now when Jesus was born in Bethlehem of Judaea in the days of Herod the king, behold, there came wise men from the east to Jerusalem, saying, Where is he that is born King of the Jews? For we have seen his star in the east, and are come to worship him.

MATTHEW 2:1–2 KJV

And is it true,
This most tremendous tale of all,
Seen in a stained-glassed window's hue,
A baby in an ox's stall?
The maker of the stars and sea
Became a child on earth for me?

SIR JOHN BETJEMAN

It's Christmastime!
It's Christmastime!
I'm so happy it's Christmastime!
Hearts are happy
and songs are gay
God's Son was born
on Christmas Day.

WANDA ROYER

More light than we can learn,
More wealth than we can treasure,
More love than we can ever earn,
More peace than we can measure,
Because one Child is born.

UNKNOWN

The Christmas message is that there is hope for a ruined humanity—hope of pardon, hope of peace with God, hope of glory—because at the Father's will Jesus Christ became poor and was born in a stable so that thirty years later He might hang on a cross.

J. I. Packer

And Mary said, My soul doth magnify the Lord, and my spirit hath rejoiced in God my Saviour.

LUKE 1:46–47 KJV

Once in royal David's city
Stood a lowly cattle shed,
Where a mother laid her baby
In a manger for His bed:
Mary was that mother mild,
Jesus Christ, her little child.

Cecil Frances Alexander

We all need wisdom....
Wisdom to choose the right paths to take in life....
Wisdom to know right from wrong...
Wisdom to see what truly matters most.
The wise men were willing to give up their homes,
Their familiar habits,
And travel far to seek wisdom....

It takes courage to set out
looking for something new.
But if we make this journey,
God will shine His light into our lives,
Like the glimmer of that long-ago star.
All we have to do is follow.

ELLYN SANNA WITH
VIOLA RUELKE GOMMER

For he himself is our peace.

EPHESIANS 2:14 NIV

Unto us a child is born!
Ne'er has earth beheld a morn,
Among all the morns of time,
Half so glorious in its prime!

Unto us a Son is given!
He has come from God's own heaven,
Bringing with Him, from above,
Holy peace and holy love.

HORATIUS BONAR

"*But you, Bethlehem, in the land of Judah, are by no means least among the rulers of Judah; for out of you will come a ruler who will shepherd my people Israel.*"

MATTHEW 2:6 NIV

Bright portals of the sky,
Embossed with sparkling stars,
Doors of eternity,
With diamantine bars,
Your arras rich uphold,
Loose all your bolts and springs,
Ope wide your leaves of gold,
That in your roofs may come the
King of kings.

William Drummond

Anyone who has seen
me has seen the Father.

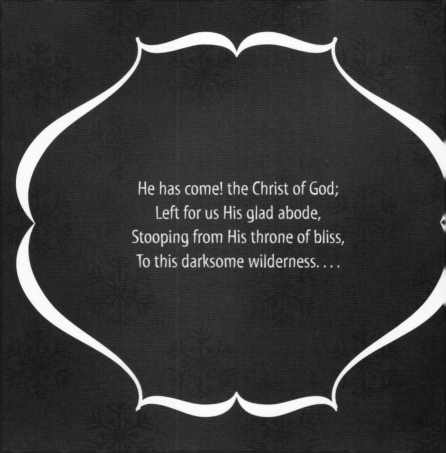

He has come! the Christ of God;
Left for us His glad abode,
Stooping from His throne of bliss,
To this darksome wilderness. . . .

He has come! the Prince of Peace;
Come to bid our sorrows cease;
Come to scatter with His light
All the darkness of our night.

HORATIUS BONAR

Hark! The herald angels sing
"Glory to the newborn King;
Peace on earth and mercy mild,
God and sinners reconciled!"
Joyful all ye nations rise,
Join the triumph of the skies;
With th' angelic host proclaim
Christ is born in Bethlehem.

CHARLES WESLEY

When we celebrate Christmas,
we are celebrating that amazing
time when the Word that shouted
all the galaxies into being, limited
all power, and for the love of us
came to us in the powerless body
of a human baby.

MADELEINE L'ENGLE

The baby born in the manger
was not only a helpless infant.
God clothed Himself in a tiny human
body—but even while Jesus was
totally human, He was also totally
God. We cannot understand this
paradox, but somehow the Christ
Child contained the Creator
of the universe. . . .

When we look at
Jesus we see who
God really is—a
being of love and
mercy and joy.

For God so loved the world that
he gave his one and only Son,
that whoever believes in him shall
not perish but have eternal life.

JOHN 3:16 NIV

A newborn baby, the child of poor parents. . .
who would have thought He could change
the entire world? If you live your life as
though you were the center of the world,
then the life of that baby threatens to shake
your being at its very foundations. But that
same baby also offers you a greater security,
a greater joy, and a greater love than
any you have ever known.

When we find our truest,
deepest selves, we find God.
And when we find God's presence,
we find our true selves.
Isn't that what Christmas
is all about?

*Give thanks to the L*ORD*, for he is good; his love endures forever.*

PSALM 118:1 NIV

Rejoice that immortal God is born, so that mortal man may live in eternity.

JOHN HUSS

Sometimes we want to give up.
God doesn't seem to answer His door.
We're tired of searching for His face.
The Christmas story seems too
good to be true, a fairy tale
meant for children. . . .

But when Jesus comes,
He makes even tired, grown-up
hearts young again. May you
feel Him touch your heart this
Christmas season and all year long.

ELLYN SANNA WITH
VIOLA RUELKE GOMMER

May Emmanuel find welcome in our hearts,
Take flesh in our lives,
And be for all peoples the welcome advent
Of redemption and grace.

THE ROMAN MISSAL

"But you, Bethlehem, in the land of Judah, are by no means least among the rulers of Judah; for out of you will come a ruler who will shepherd my people Israel."

MATTHEW 2:6 NIV

"What means this glory round our feet,"
the magi mused, "more bright than morn?"
And voices chanted clear and sweet,
"Today the Prince of Peace is born!" . . .

"What means that star,"
the shepherds said,
"that brightens through
the rocky glen?"
And angels,
answering overhead,
sang, "Peace on earth,
goodwill to men!"

JAMES RUSSELL LOWELL

The King of glory sends His Son,
To make His entrance on this earth;
Behold the midnight bright as noon,
And heav'nly hosts declare His birth! . . .

About the young Redeemer's head,
What wonders and what glories meet!
An unknown star arose and led
The eastern sages to His feet.

Isaac Watts

The magi, those kings from the East, were wise enough to set aside their own worldly power and position. Instead, they yielded their lives to the guidance of a star—and when they found the child, they bowed down and offered Him their treasures.

*Jesus Christ is the same yesterday
and today and forever.*

I rejoice in the hope of that glory to be revealed, for it is no uncertain glory that we look for. Our hope is not hung upon such an untwisted thread as, "I imagine so," or "It is likely," but the cable, the strong tow of our fastened anchor, is the oath and promise of Him who is eternal verity. Our salvation is fastened with God's own hand, and with Christ's own strength, to the strong stake of God's unchangeable nature.

SAMUEL RUTHERFORD

Christ's words are of permanent value because of His person; they endure because He endures.

W. H. GRIFFITH THOMAS

Come to Bethlehem and see Christ
whose birth the angels sing;
Come adore on bended knee, Christ
the Lord, the newborn King.
Gloria, in excelsis Deo!
Gloria, in excelsis Deo!

TRADITIONAL FRENCH CAROL

Somehow, not only at
Christmas, but all
the long year through,
the joy that you give
to others is the joy that
comes back to you.

JOHN GREENLEAF WHITTIER

Happy, happy Christmas, that can win us back to the delusions of our childhood days, recall to the old man the pleasures of his youth, and transport the traveler back to his own fireside and quiet home!

CHARLES DICKENS

*Every good and perfect
gift is from above.*

JAMES 1:17 NIV

This the month, and this the happy morn,
Wherein the Son of heaven's eternal King,
Of wedded maid and virgin mother born,
Our great redemption from above did bring. . . .

For so the holy sages once did sing,
That He our deadly forfeit should release,
And with His Father work us a perpetual peace.

JOHN MILTON

With our minds on life's looming problems. . .
we sometimes forget to notice that God's presence
has crept quietly and sweetly into the smallest
details of our lives—like the sun on our face,
a warm hand in ours, a child's laughter, and a
family's love. This Christmas season, may you see
the Christmas Baby at the heart of your life.

ELLYN SANNA WITH
VIOLA RUELKE GOMMER